WITH EVERY NOTE
I SING

G-4392

WITH EVERY NOTE
I SING

PRAYERS FOR MUSIC MINISTERS
AND THOSE WHO LOVE TO SING

DAVID HAAS

GIA PUBLICATIONS, INC.
CHICAGO

Art direction and design by Daniel Kantor and Jennifer Spong
Cover Photo courtesy of University of St. Thomas Liturgical Choir, St. Paul MN
Edited by Mary Jane Moore

Excerpt from "A Musician's Prayer" by Joe Wise,
© Copyright 1976
by the National Association of Pastoral Musicians.
Used with permission.

English translations of the Lord's Prayer,
The International Consultation on English Texts.

ISBN: 0-941050-75-0

TO JO INFANTE

TABLE OF CONTENTS

FOR THE GIFT OF PRAYER
Teach Me the Songs of Your Truth 14
Help Me to Pray 15

FOR THE MORNING
Greeting 18
Good Morning 19
A Morning Psalm...20
Canticle of Zachary 22
Hear O Israel 23

FOR THE EVENING
Greeting 26
A Prayer for the Evening...27
O Brilliant Light 28
An Evening Psalm...29
Canticle of Mary 31

BEFORE GOING TO SLEEP
Greeting 34
A Night Prayer...35
A Night Psalm...36
Canticle of Simeon 37
In Beauty We Walk 38
Hail, Holy Queen 39

BEFORE AND AFTER THE LITURGY
For the Gift of Hospitality 42
A Musician's Prayer 43
After the Liturgy..45

FOR THE JOURNEY OF THE LITURGICAL YEAR
First Sunday of Advent...48
Second Sunday of Advent 49
Immaculate Conception 50
Third Sunday of Advent 51
Fourth Sunday of Advent..52
Christmas...53
Holy Family..54
Mary, Mother of God..55
Epiphany..56

Baptism of the Lord..57
Ash Wednesday 58
First Sunday of Lent..59
Second Sunday of Lent..60
Third Sunday of Lent..61
Fourth Sunday of Lent..62
Fifth Sunday of Lent...63
Passion Sunday 64
Holy Thursday 65
Good Friday 66
The Vigil of Easter 67
Easter Sunday 69
Second Sunday of Easter...70
Third Sunday of Easter..71
Fourth Sunday of Easter 72
Fifth Sunday of Easter 73
Sixth Sunday of Easter 74
Ascension 75
Seventh Sunday of Easter 76
Pentecost...77
Trinity Sunday...78
The Body and Blood of Christ 79
Christ the King..80

FOR SPECIAL FEASTS
Assumption..82
All Saints...83
All Souls..84
Thanksgiving..85

FOR SACRAMENTS AND SPECIAL TIMES
Prayer Before Infant Baptism 88
Prayer Before the Rite of Acceptance Into the Catechumenate 89
Prayer Before the Rite of Election...90
Prayer Before a Scrutiny 91
Prayer Before a Celebration of Christian Initiation.................92
Prayer Before a Celebration of Reconciliation.........................93
Prayer Before a Celebration of Ministry 94
Prayer Before the Celebration of Marriage 95
Prayer Before an Anointing Service...96
Prayer Before a Funeral...97

MORE PRAYERS
    Prayer of Dedication 100
    Prayer Before Planning a Celebration 101
    Prayer Before a Rehearsal 102
    Prayer for Sharing and Reflecting on the Word of God............103
    Prayer to Overcome Nervousness....................................104
    Prayer for When the Voice is Gone.................................105
    Prayer for When There are Distractions...........................106
    Prayer for Healing from Apathy 107
    Prayer for When there is Conflict................................108

TABLE PRAYERS
    Bless Us, O Lord 110
    Be Present At Our Table 111
    Blessed Are You 112
    You Bring Bread 113
    The Eyes of All Hope In You 114
    Thanksgiving After the Meal 115

BLESSINGS
    The Blessing of Aaron 118
    The Blessing of Moses...119
    When We Are Out of Each Other's Sight.............................120
    May the God of Peace Be With You All 121
    That We May Walk With God 122
    May God's Peace Keep Watch Over Us 123
    The God of All Grace 124
    Irish Blessing 125
    Gospel Kindred 126
    Sufi Blessing 127

COMMON PRAYERS
    The Sign of the Cross 130
    The Lord's Prayer (Traditional)..................................131
    The Lord's Prayer (Contemporary) 132
    The Abba Prayer of Jesus and the Body of Christ 133
    Doxology 135
    The Beatitudes 136
    The Jesus Prayer..138
    The "O" Antiphons...139
    Eternal Rest..141

Come Holy Spirit...142
Stations of the Cross...143
Easter Proclamation 144
Prayer of Saint Francis 145
Prayer of Saint Patrick...146
Prayer of Saint Ignatius 147
Holy Spirit Prayer of Saint Augustine..........................148
The Serenity Prayer 149

MARIAN PRAYERS
Hail Mary 152
A Prayer to Mary...153
The Angelus..154
Regina Caeli (Queen of Heaven) 155
Memorare 156
The Mysteries of the Rosary 157

INTRODUCTION

*F*or those charged with the ministry of music, the challenge of living and nurturing one's own spiritual life can be difficult. Many (myself included) find it difficult to stop, breathe, and take the time to pray. Why? First of all, because we feel we are often too submerged in our work making sure everybody else on Sunday is able to pray, and second, we can easily make the case that our ministry is communal and relational, and therefore we should avoid anything that smacks of individualism. I know for myself, these can become convenient rationalizations in the midst of my own avoidance of the need for prayer.

Yes, as parish music ministers our primary call is to help empower the common liturgical prayer of the assembly. But to neglect our own personal spiritual conversation with God, is to abuse ourselves, and ultimately has consequences for our ministry to those whom we serve in our faith communities.

I am often asked, "how do you find time to pray?" or "how do you center yourself in order to put yourself in the right frame of mind to celebrate the liturgy?" I honestly have to admit I do not always take the time, or when I do, I find myself searching for the right thoughts to offer in prayer. But when I pause and focus well, and enter into this wonderful dialogue, I know that I need to visit that place more regularly and with a deeper commitment.

As ministers of sung prayer, the first place for us to go is to the scriptures, particularly the Psalms. The Psalter is the primal prayer book for musicians. Some of us may have a spiritual director, others take the time to make an annual retreat, and there are many other schools of prayer that speak to our different personalities, as we all have our own unique spiritual "hard wiring." What you will find in these pages are simple prayers and conversations that I have entered into with the Holy One, and with myself on my own journey of faith. Many of these prayers have been in my heart for sometime, others were created for this collection. I have also added some classics from our tradition, new versions of many of our venerable texts, and a few gems from other sources.

These are prayers for all engaged in music ministry - directors, cantors, instrumentalists, choir and ensemble members, and of course, the primary music minister, the members of the worshipping assembly. There are prayers for all times of the day; prayers to help us prepare and reflect upon our worship; prayers for the seasons, sacramental celebrations, and other events. The prayer texts are mostly written in first person, but can be easily adapted for group gatherings. It is my hope that this book can serve as a spiritual jump-start for the many busy, overworked, and committed ministers of music serving the prayer and praise of our people.

I want to thank Dan Kantor for being a treasured friend, and for his advice, honesty, and hard work on the design of this book. Thanks also to my dear friend Mary Jane Moore for her work in editing the manuscript, and for being such a wonderful presence in my life over the years. I want to thank Joe Wise, Marty Haugen, Joe Camacho, Bonnie Faber, Frank Brownstead, Sue Seid-Martin, Jim Dunning, Betsey Beckman, Jim Bessert, and Ray East for their friendship and for igniting the inspiration for some of the prayers that are found in these pages.

Thanks also to dear friends Mary Werner, Rob and Mary Glover, Bob Piercy, Jean Bross, Art and Kathy Zannoni, Stephen and Judy Petrunak, Barbara Colliander, Leon Roberts, George DeCosta, Diane Bilich, Bill Huebsch, Carole

Kastigar, Jim Moudry, Lori True, Lisa Chase, Jim Moore, Kristin Blount, Jo Mabini Greene, Vicky Tufano, Michael Bilich, Mel and Therese Harvey, Loretta Reif, Pam Cole, Carol Porter, Toni Kerker, Thom Morris, Marie Fortier, Sharon and Mark Nicpon, and Barbara Conley Waldmiller for the love and care which they lavish upon me.

Finally, I want to thank Ed and Alec Harris, Michael Cymbala, and Bob Batastini at GIA Publications for their ongoing faith in my gifts; to Leslie Bonshire, Patricia Stromen, and the associates of the Emmaus Center; to my wonderful parents; to Helen, for breathing into me a fresh presence of the power of God in the midst of confusion and questions; and especially to my life long friend, Jo Infante, for continually showing me what it means to pray with the entirety of one's life.

Soli Deo Gloria!

David Haas
The Emmaus Center for Music, Prayer, and Ministry
St. Paul, Minnesota

FOR THE GIFT
OF PRAYER

TEACH ME THE SONGS OF YOUR TRUTH

*T*each me the songs of your truth, O Lord,
that I may bear fruit in you.
Open to me the music of your spirit,
that with every note I sing,
I may praise you.
Out of your kindness grant me this.
For you are the answer to all our needs.
Alleluia! †

DH/FROM THE ODES OF SOLOMON, 2ND CENTURY

HELP ME TO PRAY

*G*od,
Help me to feel free enough to let go,
To let you take over,
To accept your presence.
Transform my ego to give way to humble service,
Set free my self-consciousness,
Lighten my worry and need to control outcomes.
Accept my prayer;
Help me to accept you.
Send me the gift of breath,
that I may greet with joy the spirit
which I know
is singing deep within my heart.

Amen. †

DH

PRAYERS FOR THE MORNING

GREETING

O Lord. open my lips,
and my mouth shall declare your praise. **†**

GOOD MORNING

*G*od,
Good morning.

Come and fill my day with new breath,
that I may be a living hymn of praise to you.

As I begin this day,
I thank you that last night was not my
last night.

For one more day,
you have given me the gift of life.
May I embrace all that you are to me,
the light from heaven and songs of the earth,
the joy of my heart,
and the hope of all my dreaming.

May your love be my calling this day,
and may I this day proclaim your power and promise.

A new day.
A new encounter with you.
A new reason to sing.

For this I give you thanks.

Amen. †

DH

A MORNING PSALM

*A*s morning breaks,
I look to you O God, to be my strength this day.

God, you are my God whom I seek,
for you my soul is thirsting.
Like a dry and waterless land,
my soul is thirsting for you.

As morning breaks,
I look to you O God, to be my strength this day.

I gaze upon you in your holy place,
to see your power and your glory.
For your love is better than life itself,
my lips will glorify you.

As morning breaks,
I look to you O God, to be my strength this day.

I will bless you all my life,
in your name I will lift up my hands in prayer.
My soul will feast as with the riches of a banquet,
my mouth shall praise you with joy.

As morning breaks,
I look to you O God, to be my strength this day. †

As I lie in bed I remember you,
I meditate on you through the night.
For you have always been my help,
and in the shadow of your wings I shout for joy.
I cling to you, and your right hand upholds me.

As morning breaks,
I look to you O God, to be my strength this day. †

DH/PSALM 62

CANTICLE OF ZACHARY

*B*lest are you, O God of Israel,
you have come to set your people free.
You raise up a song of saving power,
from the house of David your servant.
You have promised freedom from all evil,
as stories tell us from so long ago.

Mercy is your promise to us all,
the covenant remembered by your people:
We are free to worship without fear,
right and holy throughout all our days.

You, O Child, are gift and prophet for us;
you go forth to show us the way,
Singing the news of salvation
through your healing power over death.

Your morning sun will be our compassion,
breaking through the darkness of night,
Shining on the ones beneath the shadows,
and leading all to walk in your way of peace. †

DH/THE BENEDICTUS - LUKE 1:68-79

HEAR, O ISRAEL

*H*ear, O Israel!
The Lord is our God, the Lord alone!
Blessed is God's glorious kingdom for ever and ever.
You shall love the Lord, your God,
with all your mind,
with all your soul,
and with all your strength. †

SH'MA ISRAEL/DEUTERONOMY 6:4-9

PRAYERS FOR THE EVENING

GREETING

O God, come to my assistance.
O Lord, make haste to help me. †

A PRAYER FOR THE EVENING

*G*od,
You have walked with me all day,
and for this I thank you.

Once again you have loved me enough
to bring me to the end of this day safe,
and secure in your presence.

It is my prayer and hope that in all
my activities,
I gave glory to you.

Thank you for another day.
Help me greet this evening in your peace.

Amen. †

DH

O BRILLIANT LIGHT

O Brilliant light,
you are the raging sun of God Most Holy,
the eternal face of God.
Your image is the image of light,
that splashes upon your heavenly home.

O Child born
of the great source of life;
from beginning to end
we praise you.
Our voices are lifted high
as we sing the song of your holy name.

O Redeemer of all creation,
as we see the day beginning to leave us,
and as your light continues to shine,
we praise Abba with you,
and we walk in the spirit,
one in your presence. †

DH/INSPIRED FROM THE PHOS HILARON

AN EVENING PSALM

*M*y my prayers rise before you
like incense,
my hands be an evening offering to you.

Come quickly O God, I call to you!
Listen to my prayer;
May my prayer rise before you
like incense,
my hands are raised high,
like an evening sacrifice.

May my prayers rise before you
like incense,
my hands be an evening offering to you.

Set a guard over my mouth,
watch over my thoughts and words;
keep all evil from me,
may I never join the wicked at their table.

May my prayers rise before you
like incense,
my hands be an evening offering to you.

The just ones may keep me pure,
for their rebuke is kindness to me.
Let not the wicked anoint my head,
I will pray against their hateful path.

May my prayers rise before you
like incense,
my hands be an evening offering to you.

Lord my God, I turn to you,
In you I find safety and refuge.
Do not take my life from me.

May my prayers rise before you
like incense,
my hands be an evening offering to you. †

DH/PSALM 141:1-5, 8

CANTICLE OF MARY

*A*ll that I am,
sings of the God who brings new life
to birth in me.
My spirit soars on the wings of my Lord!

My soul gives glory to the Lord,
rejoicing in my saving God;
Who looks upon me in my state,
and all the world will call me blest;
For God works marvels in my sight,
and holy, holy is God's name.

God's mercy is from age to age,
on those who follow in fear;
Whose arm is power and strength
and scatters all the proud of heart;
Who casts the mighty from their thrones,
and raises up the lowly ones.

God fills the starving with good things,
the rich are left with empty hands;
Protecting all the faithful ones,
remembering Israel with mercy;
The promise known to those before,
and to their children forever. †

DH/THE MAGNIFICAT - LUKE 1:46-55

PRAYERS BEFORE GOING TO SLEEP

GREETING

*M*ay almighty God grant us a restful night
and a peaceful death. †

A NIGHT PRAYER

*G*od,
Thank you for the mystery of the night,
the home and holder of dreams.
Nourish the upcoming sleep with stories
of the depth of your love.
May the wonderful images that lie ahead
dream a new vision of your love.
Thank you for the gift of stars,
the brightness of the moon,
and all the sounds of night.

Help me not be fearful of the night,
but embrace it as the center of peace.
May I hold the silence - which is the best music of all;
Because it is there where some of the finest melodies
are sung;
It is there where you dwell most clearly,
and where you call me most honestly
to live in faithfulness to you.

Good night.

Amen. †

DH

A NIGHT PSALM

*L*ike a little child in its mother's arms,
my soul will rest in you.

My heart is not proud, my eyes do not seek
the ways from above; the things that are great.
The marvels beyond are not what I need,
for you are my peace.

Like a little child in its mother's arms,
my soul will rest in you.

Quiet and still, my soul is calm,
in your sweet embrace, like mother and child.
My hope is in you; my heart is full
for you are my peace.

Like a little child in its mother's arms,
my soul will rest in you. †

DH/PSALM 131

CANTICLE OF SIMEON

*N*ow, O Holy One,
you can dismiss your servant in peace;
you have kept your promise,
you have fulfilled your word.

My eyes have seen your saving power
which you have made known for all to see:

A light to reveal you to all nations,
and the glory of your people Israel. †

DH/NUNC DIMITIS LUKE 2:29-30

IN BEAUTY WE WALK

*I*n beauty we walk;
with beauty before us, we walk.
with beauty behind us, we walk.
with beauty above us, we walk.
with beauty above us and about us, we walk.
It is finished in beauty. †

A NAVAJO NIGHT CHANT

HAIL, HOLY QUEEN

*H*ail, holy Queen, Mother of mercy!
Hail, our life, comfort and hope!
To you do we cry, poor banished children of Eve.
To you do we send up our sighs,
mourning and weeping in this vale of tears.
Turn then, most gracious advocate,
your eyes of mercy toward us;
and after this, our exile,
show unto us the blessed fruit of your womb,
Jesus.
O clement, O loving, O sweet Virgin Mary!
Amen. †

SALVE REGINA

PRAYERS BEFORE AND AFTER THE LITURGY

FOR THE GIFT OF HOSPITALITY

*G*od,
Open the doors wide,
unlock the barriers
of my apathy, my judgement,
and my fear.

Set me free from my place of comfort,
to go out of my way, to inconvenience myself,
to leave the solace of my own world.

Bless me once again with the gift you have given me,
outstretch your loving embrace through my own arms,
to welcome those whom you call your children.

Help my eyes be your eyes, who awaken the weary;
that I may see the wonderful treasure that they are,
and give freely the gifts that you have given to me.

May I welcome others,
as you have welcomed me
again and again,
as the eternal, impeccable host.

May it never be the case,
that there be strangers in this place.

Amen. †

DH

A MUSICIAN'S PRAYER

*Q*uiet
God I need this quiet
before you
before me
before we begin
to settle
to touch base, and space
and pace
that is more fully human
more fully you
to chamois off
the dull haze
of routine ...

Sunday morning services,
Lord, they
always come after
Saturday nights
the heads and tongues
are thick and dry
Let me go slow
go real
to where we are
go with the old
the young, the not so sure
Go easy
appear and disappear
lead and be led
in the flow....

let me be quick
to hand over
the quest
for your presence
and ours to each other
to all of us

Help us get inside
the rhythms today Lord
Really inside
core out the words
taste, touch and handle
them as once we did
with your best word
Trigger our inner journeys
Invest us in our tunes
Squander us on your word
Lay us out
rainbowed
voice to voice
face to face
drummer boy
Best for you
Best for them
Best for us †

EXCERPTED FROM A PRAYER BY JOE WISE

AFTER THE LITURGY

*G*od,
Thank you.

I thank you for the community who gathered together,
with the many faces and manifestations
of your presence.

I thank you for the many people
who served in the many ministries,
who gave of their talents to serve your people.

I thank you for the hymns and songs,
so wonderfully prayed and sung for your glory.

I thank you for the gift of your saving Word,
for planting your seed within us.

I thank you for the gift of your most sacred meal,
for sharing with you most intimately at your table.

And I thank you for the mission
that you have called all of us to accept -
to be your life for the world.

For this I give thanks.

Amen. †

DH

PRAYERS FOR THE
JOURNEY OF
THE LITURGICAL YEAR

FIRST SUNDAY OF ADVENT

*G*od,
You are the Shepherd and keeper of my life.
Come, awaken and rouse your power within me.
Take care of the voice and praise that you
have instilled in me;
That I may sing of the hope
that comes from your Word.

Help me to stay awake
and be on the watch for you;
Open my eyes to see the signs of your coming;
Fill me with kindness to proclaim your eternal justice;
Help me to forever turn to you,
to the strength of your song,
as I pray and sing on behalf of all who long
for your presence.
Now and for always.

Amen. †

DH

SECOND SUNDAY OF ADVENT

*G*od,
You are the comfort and tenderness that I seek;
From your hand I know your mercy, justice, and peace.
Once again, you have called me
like your messenger before you,
to proclaim your way;
To make clear the highway,
singing forever upon your mountain,
Crying out the good news!
Announcing your coming,
with all the strength that I can muster,
the power and glory which is yours.

For I have seen the great things
you have done for your people;
When I have drowned in my own tears,
you have taken me by the hand to dry land,
rejoicing!

For salvation continues to come from your promise.

Amen. †

DH

IMMACULATE CONCEPTION

God,
You have showered upon me the
blessing from heaven,
and you have chosen me
and called me to holiness.

You have known me before I was born,
and you have a plan for me.

Like Mary,
may I be open to the path
that you have set before me.
Help me to respond,
not in fear,
but rather with the song of faith.

I am your servant,
let it be done to me as you say.

Amen. †

DH

THIRD SUNDAY OF ADVENT

*G*od,
You are always faithful,
always just,
always by my side.

How can I keep from singing?
My soul is filled with your love and compassion,
and you have honored me
with the music of your coming.

May the lowly sing your goodness;
May the brokenhearted know
the healing phrases of your creation;
May those who are imprisoned
join in the hymn of new freedom;
May the ministry that you have entrusted to me
be like your justice,
which rains down on the meadow,
like the showers that water the earth.
May I rejoice in you always,
and know your peace.

Amen. †

DH

FOURTH SUNDAY OF ADVENT

*G*od,
You are the great author of my life;
I welcome you.

How can I possibly ascend
to the height of your mountain?
How can I possibly stand in your place,
in your holy sanctuary?
As your messenger,
help my hands reach out to those in need,
free my voice to be your blessing,
seek me,
so I may seek your face,
and may the psalms and songs I cry out today
fill the longing of every human heart:

Maranatha! Come, Lord Jesus!

Amen. †

DH

CHRISTMAS

*G*od,
You are the light of the World;
you have chosen to become like us,
walk with us,
and be hope for all
who stumble through the terror of life.

You are with us here! Gloria in Excelsis!

How can I thank you for such a gift?
How can I possibly sing a song worthy enough
and beautiful enough to match your glory?

All I can do is seek you with all my heart,
rely on your power,
open myself to your love,
which melts away the chill,
the bitterness,
and the cold
that can still find a home in me.
Be born again in my life,
and fire within me "love's pure light."
May the music be loud and joyful,
now and forever.

Amen. †

DH

HOLY FAMILY

*G*od,
As I grow, I am often tempted to move
far away from my family -
whatever that family may be:
my parents,
my brothers and sisters,
my spouse, my children, my friends,
or my parish family.
I am even sometimes arrogant enough to think
that I do not need you.

Help me not to isolate myself,
help me to lean on others,
to be present and attentive,
to bear with others in my life
graced with patience,
and be faithful to the baptism
which makes me one with them
and with you.
You call us as your children;
may I run to you,
please do not forget to scoop me up into your arms,
hold me close,
and teach me your song.

May there be many family reunions.

Amen. †

DH

MARY, MOTHER OF GOD

God,
I thank you for giving me heroes.

Mary bore your presence into the world,
and lived her "yes"
to perfection.

I ask you to help me God,
to make her response - my response:
to live with strength
and obedience,
and to share with humility
the joy of my heart
with your people-
who are the joy of your heart.

Amen. †

DH

EPIPHANY

*G*od,
Today I celebrate the many ways
you are made known to me.

I ask you to always be my guiding star.
I pledge to try to follow your light in faith
as I stand to lead and serve your people.

May all of us who gather to worship this day
be people of welcome and warmth;
be the presence of joy in your Word;
be the ongoing "gift" of your incarnation;
and be the people who you have called
to dance in the glory of your light.

Amen. ✝

DH

BAPTISM OF THE LORD

*G*od,
You constantly call and form us to be your people.
To open blind eyes;
to release those who are imprisoned;
and pull each other free from the dungeon of darkness.

You have called me to be your servant,
your chosen one.
Continue to fill me with your spirit,
as we sing together the dream of justice on the earth.

Help this community of faith to be the best it can be,
to be the beacon of service and mission to the world,
to take up our cross,
to die and rise again and again,
to become your "church."

Amen. †

DH

ASH WEDNESDAY

*G*od,
Again you call us to return to you,
for now is the time,
today our salvation is promised to us!

Cleanse me God,
wash me from all that keeps me far from you.
Do not hide your face,
keep your spirit around and within me

You call on me to sing
of your mercy and reconciliation,
to be the presence of Christ.
You mark me with your cross.

May this Lent truly be your "springtime,"
and may our music be the sun and water
necessary to nurture the Easter we long for.

Amen. †

DH

FIRST SUNDAY OF LENT

*G*od,
You are our beginning ánd our end.
You give us this time,
not of shame, guilt, and pain,
but a time of fulfillment and growth.

Help me to set my thoughts on your compassion,
help me to focus on your saving Word;
help my singing today,
may it sing of a life that flows
from the cross of Christ,
dwelling on your promise of new life from death.

Amen. †

DH

SECOND SUNDAY OF LENT

*G*od,
Time and time again you have shown us
a glimpse of your glory;
And yet, each time, you summon each of us
to return to the everyday life of broken promises.

Help me to see your hope in all this;
May the dazzling miracle of your splendor
keep me going forward without cynicism.

For I know and believe
that the miracles you send
are signs of our ultimate destiny and promise.

Today I sing and rejoice,
 believing that it truly is
"Good to be here" with you.

Amen. †

DH

THIRD SUNDAY OF LENT

*G*od,
Nothing can be kept from you,
for you know me better than I know myself.

May the music that sings forth today,
be living water for all who thirst for you.
May the song in my heart
continue to name you as Messiah;
May the sound from my lips
proclaim you as the Savior of the world.

Amen. †

DH

FOURTH SUNDAY OF LENT

*G*od,
We are pilgrims on our journey to you,
and we have no choice but to move onward.
We crawl toward you, inch by inch,
always seeking to return to your light.

How can we sing your song in a foreign land?

May I never forget you;
May I never forget
that you are sight for all who long to see.
May I seek you in all things,
and set you high above my deepest joy.
May my song be played upon the
harp of your compassion,
and fall upon the ears
and within the hearts
of your people.

Amen. †

DH

FIFTH SUNDAY OF LENT

*G*od,
You are marvelous, indeed!
You love me so much,
that you are willing
to crawl into my tomb,
embrace the stench,
and free me from the shame of my existence.

You journey toward me,
and you weep for me,
and yet you are
unwilling to let me stay
in the "safety" of the smell.
You call me to rise up.
Your song deafens the voices of fear
that I coddle within myself.

You are really serious about life from death.

Help me to have the courage to not stay put,
hiding in the dark of death;
Free me from the bondage
that keeps me enslaved.
Unlock the symphony that proclaims
"God to the rescue!"

Amen. ✝

DH

PASSION SUNDAY

God,
Blessed be the one who comes
in your name!

Today we all begin the journey of your passion,
and you call me to live the story with you.
Help me to stay attentive,
and to listen well.

May I sing and pray with the obedience of Christ,
and together with him,
raise up to glory with you.

May that same humility fill my voice
and my heart.
May I take on your form,
and to be like you.
May I understand more deeply
the gift of suffering,
and thus sing the eternal music in praising you.

Amen. †

DH

HOLY THURSDAY

God,
Tonight we gather to glory in your cross,
to share in your salvation.

How shall I make a return to you?
Your love and goodness is unfathomable,
too rich and vast.
No song, no choir,
no arrangement of sound can come close
to matching the beauty of your name.

All you ask of me is to serve your people,
to wash their feet,
to bring a message of hope to the poor,
to proclaim liberty to those who are held captive,
to bring sight to the blind,
and proclaim your command:
"as I have done, so you must do."

I must do more than break and share in the bread,
I must be totally open
to be broken
for the sake of my brothers and sisters.

Make it so, God.
Make it so.

Amen. †

DH

GOOD FRIDAY

*G*od,
You have not forgotten us,
for you continue to remember our plight.
You restore us,
and make us whole
over and over again.

Your strange method of
blood, nails, and the cross,
provide the the most wonderful identity
that we could imagine:
"No longer abandoned."

I too will journey with you
on the way that you walked,
I will sing the lament,
remembering your passion,
and the pledge of your resurrection.

Come close, O God,
and mark me
with the sign of your cross.
May all your people fly with you
in the shadow of your wings,
singing for joy!

Amen. †

DH

THE VIGIL OF EASTER

*G*od,
This is your most holy night.

We feel the warmth and terror of the fire,
the fire that not only lightens up the night,
but a blaze that we hope will torch the world
of all that is evil,
all that is filled with hate,
all that is seduced by the need to make war,
all that is poisoned by violence and darkness.

This is your most holy night.
We listen to the stories of beginnings,
but they are more than the first act,
they are the entire drama,
your history within our history,
unfolding and bringing forth
the heavenly power of your Word.

This is your most holy night.
We are almost drowned
by the surging water splashing about,
the sprinklers set high,
seeping deep into the cracks of our dry land,
refreshing and bringing new color to the canvas,
creating us anew,
your wonderful work of art.

This is your most holy night.
We are filled with the aroma of your anointing,
glistening,
pouring and dripping down our faces,
travelling through the pores of our skin
and making a home
within the boundaries of our souls.
You robe us in royalty and glory,
with a fragrance that will always remain.

This is your most holy night.
We are honored by the blessing of a sacred meal,
huge portions,
family style,
enough for everyone.
This banquet is beyond sustenance,
but more the tease and promise of the
greatest feast of all -
the table of your kingdom.

This is your most holy night.
We are awed and humbled by this night,
a night like which there is no other;

We ask that you take and mold us,
Sing in us the glory of your Christ,
risen, now and forever!

Amen. †

DH

EASTER SUNDAY

*G*od,
This is the day!
You have made it good!
I rejoice in you!

Today is the promise of fear being shattered,
Today is the promise of the cold melting away,
Today is the promise of graves opened
and tombs emptied,
Today is the promise of prisoners freed,
Today is the promise of hope,
Today is the promise of dried tears,
Today is the promise of forgiveness and healing,
Today is the promise of lies being whisked away,
Today is the promise of music and dancing,
Today is the promise of life!
Today!
Your day!
Ours to share!

I rejoice in you!

Amen. †

DH

SECOND SUNDAY OF EASTER

*G*od,
You are the dazzling light
that keeps me lucid,
focused,
and filled with possibilities.

Light of light,
shine above,
below,
behind and in front of me,
and may the power of your resurrection
be the source of life within me.

Keep the songs clear and not blurred;
keep the voice steady in the faith
that your wonderful gift of life provides.

Alleluia!

Amen. †

DH

THIRD SUNDAY OF EASTER

God,
You are the love that welcomes all to joy;
You fill my soul with happiness beyond
anything I have known before.

Draw near to me,
stay close to me.

You have taken my hand
and given me the wings to fly
beyond the limitations of myself.
For you have given me
the intimacy of knowing you,
and there is no greater gift.

May the gift of my music sing forever
of your outstanding and lavish love for me,
and may my voice share the story
of how I have risen with you.

Alleluia!

Amen. †

DH

FOURTH SUNDAY OF EASTER

*G*od,
Your rising is like the mighty wind,
and your wisdom
like the high waves of the sea.

You have shown the power of life in all things,
and for this I praise you with my entire being.
You have saved my soul from death,
and have given me a new spirit,
a new life!

May I never cease in praising you,
may I drum with delight,
and dance with abandon!

For you are the God who loves me, no matter what!

Alleluia!

Amen. †

DH

FIFTH SUNDAY OF EASTER

*G*od,
Your presence can be seen
in the beautiful colors of your creation.
Time and time again,
without repeating yourself,
you create and invent wonders
that are dazzling to the eyes.

The spring is filled with the blossoms and flowers,
all the green things are coming up strong,
the snow and frost have given way
to the budding of your indescribable splendor.

You are my joy and my feast,
the God of so many surprises!

May my praising of you
proclaim the newborn patterns of your handiwork,
and may all who worship you
see their own resurrection.

Alleluia!

Amen. †

DH

SIXTH SUNDAY OF EASTER

*G*od,
In you I find the garden of paradise,
the smell and fragrance of your presence
fills my senses,
and makes your home within me.

I thank you God,
for being the God that I have longed for.
I have seen you,
I have heard your voice,
and I know you are alive.

May those whom I serve,
see you in my eyes,
hear your voice in my music,
and come to be filled with the everlasting
peace that comes in following you.

Alleluia!

Amen. †

DH

ASCENSION

*G*od,
You are the mighty and wonderful
source of all things.
You are my strength and I praise you.

When I look up to the heavens,
I see only you,
and I sing the song of joy
that only you can bring forth in me.

May my ministry be a full blown
trumpet blast,
filled with singing,
clapping,
and shouts of joy!

Alleluia!

Amen. †

DH

SEVENTH SUNDAY OF EASTER

God,
Because of your love,
I am no longer alien to you,
you have made me a part of your family,
you have called me home.

You have made me holy,
and called me to share in your dwelling,
and to share myself
as a living sacrifice of praise.

Thank you for the gift of music,
which you have given to unite your people.
May I always keep you at the center of my talents,
for without you I am nothing.

Alleluia!

Amen. †

DH

PENTECOST

God,
You are the Great Spirit,
the source of dreams and prophecy,
the vision of life and love,
the beginning and end,
and all that I know in between.

Shine within me the mighty rays of your light,
and break open the source of your mercy in my soul.
For I am poor, O God,
come and parent my poverty with your love.

You are tenderness and comfort to me,
my soul's most welcomed guest;
You are sweetness and grace.

I ask you today to heal my wounds,
and lavish me with strength,
melt away the walls that keep me from being at peace,
save me from the bondage of myself,
guide my steps, and keep me faithful.

Give me the music of your spirit.
May the muse infused in me
break forth like the dawn,
and fill me with a joy that will never end.

Amen. ✝

DH

TRINITY SUNDAY

God,
You are profound in your mystery,
and you never cease to amaze me;
I sometimes come to think that I have you figured out,
and then you zap me,
and remind me
that you are beyond
the limitations of my insight.

Help me to see a "thicker slice."
You are Father and Mother,
I know,
you are Son and Spirit,
yes,
but yet so much more.

As I search for the words,
titles, songs and images
that attempt to corner you,
help me to know that you are beyond my words,
deeper than any effort to be "inclusive,"
because what really matters,
is that you exist
and that I see you present in your people.

Amen. †

DH

THE BODY AND BLOOD OF CHRIST
(CORPUS CHRISTI)

*G*od,
Today I praise you,
for again you have held true to your promise,
and delivered me to the treasure
of your life giving presence.

You have taken,
blest, broken and shared
in the meal of your covenant with us.
You continually sit down with us,
and feed us with the gift of yourself.

How I long to share in the banquet of your kingdom;
but until then,
may I always take on your form,
and be the food and drink
that will nourish and satisfy
all who long to sing
your unending hymn of praise.

May I sing forever with you in the land of the living,
where your covenant will be complete.

Amen. †

DH

CHRIST THE KING

*G*od,
In you there is power and glory,
and the whole world sings your praise!

You are the continuous thread
imbedded in my back and forth ways,
you have been there,
at my beginnings and endings,
in my joys and my sorrows,
you reign over all that I have known,
all that I am,
all that I am called to be.

You are the center of my life.
Help me to see beyond my world,
and my vision.
Pull me forward through the mirage
of this time and place,
to join with you in the eternal dance
of your kingdom,
of the new world
that you have created for me
and for all who seek you.

You are the truth,
give me the strength to sing beyond the lies.

Amen. †

DH

PRAYERS FOR
SPECIAL FEASTS

ASSUMPTION

*G*od,
Happy and blest are we!

My being proclaims your greatness,
my spirit finds joy in your saving ways,
for you continue to name me
as your blessed and chosen one;
You call me to sing for all people
of your eternal mercy,
of the power you have shown,
of the hungry you have fed,
and to proclaim
how you are the fountain of all blessing.

My spirit soars -
free to follow you,
with the reminder
that your Word will be fulfilled.

May I always hold and keep your Word.

Amen. †

DH

ALL SAINTS

*G*od,
You are the living One,
Holy and strong.

How I long to see your face!

For in you I can see the fullness of the earth,
the glory of the seas,
and the awesome wonder of your holy mountain.

Everyday you call me to be like you,
to see you as you are,
to give freely with generosity
to those who are in need of hospitality.
You call me to keep your love
a secret no longer,
to proclaim the hope that you gave to all -
to the poor and the sorrowing,
to the lowly and hungry,
to those who are pure of heart,
to those who seek peace,
and to those who suffer
for the sake of your dream.

Help my life spring forth "rejoicing,"
and sing forever of the heaven that awaits us all.

Amen. †

DH

ALL SOULS

*G*od,
You are the promise of new life
to those who wait for you.

I ask you to remember those people
in my life who have died -
I know you are with them,
and I thank you
for who they were to me in my life,
and how they still are here,
in my memories,
my thoughts,
and in my secret corners
where they always seem to find me.

They are always in my heart,
and often when I sing,
I sing for them.

I pray to you,
and ask you to renew them in their life with you,
and in their ongoing life with me.
May I and all who live,
be gifted with your forgiveness
and the same promise of eternal light and peace.

Amen. †

DH

THANKSGIVING

*G*od,
How do I begin?
How do I sing of the goodness
that you have showered upon me?

I am overwhelmed by your love and mercy,
and humbled by your faithfulness to me.

There are so many things
to be thankful for:
I can see,
I can walk,
I can hear,
I can sing....

The well is deep
and brimming forth with your blessings.

You know my heart,
and I know that if the only prayer I prayed to you
were "thanks,"
that would be enough.

Thank you, God.

Amen. †

DH

PRAYERS FOR SACRAMENTS AND SPECIAL TIMES

A PRAYER BEFORE INFANT BAPTISM

*G*od,
You have done it again!

A tiny, new creation has arrived on the scene,
and you overwhelm us
with the uniqueness of each new wonder child.

A new life,
another chance for us as well -
a "wake up call" to your power!
We sing of your great work of art!

May we all gather around this child,
act silly,
make faces and tickle,
flash pictures and videos,
make merry,
and take turns in holding and rocking gently
this magical creature that has come to us
almost from nowhere.

I do not know if this child can hear my singing,
and the acclamations of joy that we share-
but for our sake I do know this:
that when those little fingers wrap around my finger-
I feel your presence.

Amen. †

DH

A PRAYER BEFORE THE RITE OF
ACCEPTANCE INTO THE CATECHUMENATE

*G*od,
It can be very scary and difficult
to make the first steps to you.

We pray for those who need the courage
to walk with you in faith,
to trust in your Word
and in the power of the cross.

Support all of us when we fall,
keep us close to you.

You say to all of us,
"come and see,"
with no assurances,
except that you will not leave us orphaned.

Blessed are they,
and blessed are we
who have the strength to follow you.

May my gift of music
help sing and dance
these brave sojourners to the family of your church,
and may all of us process and march together
to your Holy Jerusalem.

Amen. †

DH

PRAYER BEFORE THE RITE OF ELECTION

*G*od,
we believe you have called
each of us by name,
and have chosen us as your disciples.

Remember all of us whose names
are indelibly inscribed in your book of life;
may those who are about to put their
"name on the line,"
do so with our prayer, fidelity, and support.

I ask you God,
to lead me onward as well;
for you have also called me to a special purpose-
to provide the rhythms and sounds
that will pulse deeply within your people,
to sing the songs of your saving way.

May the movements of my voice,
help pave the journey forward
for all who long for your Easter.

Amen. †

DH

PRAYER BEFORE A SCRUTINY

*G*od,
We believe that you are the one
who saves us,
you shatter the graves of death and sin,
you sweep away our fear,
and purify our hearts.

Create in us clean hearts, O God -
not only those who are in the midst
of their search for you,
but all of us,
for we are all in need of purifying water,
we all cry out to have our eyes opened,
and we all need to be freed from the tomb of darkness.

We cry out to you,
the one who defies death,
the one who will shine forth a new destiny for us!

For you alone can restore us!
You alone can rescue us!

May this journey of our lament
be transformed into the promise of hope in your rising.

Amen. †

DH

PRAYER BEFORE A CELEBRATION OF CHRISTIAN INITIATION

*G*od,
We give you glory and praise,
for our brothers and sisters
who will pass through your waters of life,
be drenched in your oil of gladness,
and who will feast at the table of life.

Bless them this day O God,
and may we dance with them,
and with you,
for they have been your witness
and light to all of us.

How I see myself in them!
I am inspired by their
new and fresh faith -
help me to stay alive
in your promise of life-giving water;
May I sing forever,
and evangelize with joy
of your Christ,
risen and living among us,
forever and ever!

Amen. †

DH

PRAYER BEFORE A CELEBRATION OF RECONCILIATION

*G*od,
Help us to discover and name our failings;
the true things that often are kept hidden from us;
help us to see within ourselves
the goodness, beauty, and truth
that we are usually so quick to see in others;
the darkness which can gnaw away at our hearts,
the pain that stands in the way of healing,
the struggle which dazes us - keeps our footing off balance,
and our sins of ignorance that arise from our fear.

I call and sing to you -
may your music help all of us cross the line over to you.

Strengthen me with courage
to walk through the din and darkness,
so I may truly meet the lies and deceit,
the ugliness and the hurt, and have you embrace it fully.
May I sing and dance my humanity
to the glory of the light;
for I know that you are always quick to forgive,
but I can be so reluctant to forgive myself,
and to forgive others.
Help me to walk with your tenderness by my side,
and your healing deep within my heart.
May I always forgive and help heal the world.

Amen. †

DH

PRAYER BEFORE A CELEBRATION
OF MINISTRY

*G*od,
You are too much for me.
I find it difficult to stand in your presence
and serve you.

You keep calling me - and all your people -
to go out into the trenches and serve.

How do I serve you?
How can I possibly be worthy of your trust?

There have been so many before me
who also were doubtful:
Moses - he didn't speak too well,
Jeremiah was too young,
David was too short,
and Peter,
well, he so often "missed the boat."

I have so many limitations,
and yet, you call even still.

I have neither silver nor gold.
All I have is my heart, and my voice,
and with the help of your spirit,
I will make music to you, while I live.

Amen. †

DH

PRAYER BEFORE THE CELEBRATION
OF MARRIAGE

*G*od,
You have called woman and man
to become "one flesh."
There can be no greater of sign
of your love for us.

Send your spirit, O God,
upon those today who come forward
to passionately proclaim their love for each other.

May they always remember
that the energy and power source of their relationship
lies in their fidelity and commitment to you.

May they inspire all of us
who gather at this celebration,
to pledge ourselves more deeply to our own promises,
and our own vows to live in love.

Bless me God,
that I may be the minstrel of love songs,
and play upon my harp your grand composition,
your "Word made flesh."

May these two lovers
dance to the music of Christ.

Amen. †

DH

PRAYER BEFORE AN ANOINTING SERVICE

*G*od,
I believe that you are the great healer.
Why then, do you allow people to become sick?

Why do some get well, while others do not?
Is sickness a punishment for our sin?

It is not enough to accept all of this a "mystery,"
that's not good enough.

But in the midst of all of this, you ask us to trust you,
to believe and accept that you are a loving presence,
and that any punishment we feel
is a punishment we are inflicting upon ourselves.

Help me to understand
that this sacrament is about peace;
it is about the peace in knowing
that you are the one who orders creation,
and that I am a part of that great movement.
I am on my way, as we all are,
to understand your plan for us.

I have often heard that music can heal -
help the notes on the page become a balm
of gentleness and peace for all who pray today.

Amen. †

DH

PRAYER BEFORE A FUNERAL

*G*od,
This is where our delusions of grandeur
come to a screeching halt.

It seems as though the ending
comes quickly.

Sometimes death seems to be a blessing,
when someone suffers a long and difficult illness
- like cancer or AIDS,
and sometimes it is sudden and tragic
and our disbelief kicks us right in the face
with a numbing power.

Either way,
it is still an empty feeling,
and the loss is still felt.

As we gather to "celebrate" this funeral,
you give us the ultimate test of what we believe.
Help us to not lose heart,
help us to see that even though
death, pain, and suffering are still with us,
these things will not win,
they will not be the last word,
they will not be our destiny.

Strengthen our faith,
help us to not isolate,
but rather,

feel the pain and loss
as Jesus felt for Lazarus.
May we turn our emptiness
into the fullness of your new world,
where tears will be wiped away,
and where we will live with you forever.

Amen. †

DH

MORE PRAYERS

PRAYER OF DEDICATION

My song will be for you forever,
You, the music in my heart;
For your love is all around me,
and your goodness, always here.

You have clothed me in your promise,
You, my love, my light, my friend.
You, the way and path before me,
You will lead and guide me home.

I am here to be your servant,
You anoint me with your love.
You will hold me in my longing,
All my hope in your embrace.

With your voice you sing within me,
You, the one who knows me well.
You, my joy, my life and blessing;
When you call, you know my name.

I will pledge my love forever,
I will call your name out loud.
I will reach my hand out to you,
and I know you'll reach for me.

My song will be for you forever,
You, the music in my heart. †

DH

100

PRAYER BEFORE PLANNING
A CELEBRATION

God,
You are wonderful and great,
and you fill us with joy!

We ask that you center our hearts
and our thoughts,
as we humbly encounter your Word.
May your spirit of wisdom come to us
as we make the many choices
to help make your presence
- which is always here -
become more real for your people.

Bless this time, and instill in us
a spirit of prayerful preparation.
May our decisions be transformed
into a celebration proclaiming you,
breaking forth among us!

Come to us now.

Amen. †

DH

PRAYER BEFORE A REHEARSAL

*G*od,
I thank you with all my heart,
that you have blest me with the gift of music.

Help me to always remember
that this ministry is important and special,
and that I must always prepare well
so that the notes and words on the page
become the song within my heart.

Help me and my fellow music ministers
remember that we are not just rehearsing music,
but we are also preparing to worship you
in spirit and truth.

Amen. †

DH

PRAYER FOR SHARING AND REFLECTING ON THE WORD OF GOD

Open our minds to know you, Lord;
Open our ears to hear your voice;
Open our hearts now to your Word;
Come to us now, O Lord, our God. †

DH

THIS PRAYER MAY BE SUNG TO THE TUNE OF
"PRAISE GOD FROM WHOM ALL BLESSINGS FLOW."

PRAYER TO OVERCOME NERVOUSNESS

*G*od,
Help me to slow down,
to breathe deeply,
to think simply,
to pray softly and gently,
stop the rush of fear,
and replenish it with your peace.

Help me to remember
that you are always at my side.

Then my heart can create anew.

Amen. †

DH

104

PRAYER FOR WHEN THE VOICE IS GONE

*G*od,
It's gone, I feel half alive without my voice.
Perhaps it was because of too much singing,
or too much talking, too loud, too long, too much.

I have not been taking care of myself.
not enough sleep, not eating well,
working myself too hard.
When I am this way, I feel fearful and lonely,
for I feel I have lost my best self.

Perhaps you are once again helping me
to remember who I am, and who you are.
Help me to be still,
to not become too anxious,
and trust your presence in the midst of this absence.

May I remember that while
my vocal cords may be hoarse,
my heart is strong and filled with your presence.
Help me to sing the song
that is deep and sometimes hidden,
that does not require the larynx or the vocal folds,
or the breath of my lungs.
Release the song within my heart,
and accept with grace, not my voice - but yours.

Amen. †

DH

PRAYER FOR WHEN THERE ARE DISTRACTIONS

*G*od,
I can't clear my head,
there are distractions every where -
noises around,
and I feel preoccupied with things beyond myself:
my worries,
stress at home and at work,
too much to do....

Help me accept these distractions,
and to remember that I am human.
You call people to serve you
who are the same as everyone else.
Help these distractions keep me in touch
with the people who have come to celebrate today,
for they too are probably distracted.
So why should I be any different?

Help me to see that we are all in this together,
to be gentle with myself -
then the distractions can fall away to back burners,
and I will see only you,
and then feel freed to sing and pray
with my brothers and sisters.

Amen. ✝

DH

PRAYER FOR HEALING FROM APATHY

*G*od,
I'm sorry, but right now I really do not want to be here.
I'm not in the mood, I'm tired and bored with all of this,
I have been playing and singing
these same acclamations and responses over and over.

It's Sunday, and there are other things I'd rather be doing.
I feel guilty and ashamed of my feelings-
I like to think of myself as being altruistic about all of this.

Help me to accept where I am at, as I know you do.
I need you to get me through this,
to find ways to take better care of myself,
and find more time for leisure and play.
Help me to find time to nurture
my own spiritual life,
instead of spending all of my time
taking care of everyone else.

Help me to realize that liturgy and ministry
is sometimes ordinary and boring,
not always high stimulation and inspiration.
If I accept that and accept myself, I can get by.
Thank you for the boredom,
for it makes the "high" moments
of my ministry much greater.

Amen. †

DH

PRAYER FOR WHEN THERE IS CONFLICT

*G*od,
Things are not good right now,
people are not talking to each other,
the lines are being drawn,
turfs are being established,
and power is being sought after fiom all sides.

We are in need of your healing.

Come now,
without delay,
and soften the hardness
that people are holding within themselves,
and toward each other.

Help me to be an agent of your reconciliation.
Help me to listen well,
and bring about not "winners and losers,"
but consensus and mutual care for the parish.

May I and the others in the parish music ministry
always remember that we are called
to nurture and uphold each other,
not destroy one another.
Help us to remember why we are here.
Help us all to pray.

Amen. †

DH

TABLE PRAYERS

BLESS US, O LORD

*B*less us, O Lord, and these your gifts which we are about to receive from your goodness. Through Christ our Lord.

Amen. †

BE PRESENT AT OUR TABLE

*B*e present at our table, Lord.
Be here and everywhere adored.
Thy creatures bless and grant that we
May feast in Paradise with thee.

We thank you, Lord, for this our food,
For life and health and every good;
By your own hand may we be fed:
Give us each day our daily bread.

Amen. †

THIS PRAYER MAY BE SUNG TO THE TUNE OF
"PRAISE GOD FROM WHOM ALL BLESSINGS FLOW."

BLESSED ARE YOU

*B*lessed are you, Lord our God,
Ruler of the universe,
for you bring forth bread from the earth. †

ANCIENT JEWISH TABLE BLESSING

YOU BRING BREAD

*Y*ou bring bread from the earth
and wine to gladden our hearts. †

PSALM 104: 14

THE EYES OF ALL HOPE IN YOU

*T*he eyes of all hope in you, O God,
and you give us food in due season.
You open your hand,
and every creature is filled with your blessings. †

PSALM 104: 27-28

THANKSGIVING AFTER THE MEAL

We give you thanks for all your benefits,
almighty God,
who lives and reigns for ever and ever.

Amen. †

BLESSINGS

THE BLESSING OF AARON

*T*he Lord bless you and keep you!
The Lord let his face shine upon you
and be gracious to you!
The Lord look upon you kindly
and give you peace! †

NUMBERS 6:22-27

THE BLESSING OF MOSES

*M*ay you be blessed in the city,
and blessed in the country!
Blessed be the fruit of your womb,
the produce of your soil
and the offspring of your livestock,
the issue of your herds and the young of your flocks!
Blessed be your grain bin and your kneading bowl!
May you be blessed in your coming in,
and blessed in your going out! †

DEUTERONOMY 28:3-6

119

WHEN WE ARE OUT OF EACH
OTHER'S SIGHT

*M*ay the Lord keep watch between you and me when we are out of each other's sight. †

GENESIS 31:49

MAY THE GOD OF PEACE BE WITH YOU ALL

*M*ay our God,
who is the foundation of all patience
and encouragement,
enable us to live in perfect harmony with one another
according to the spirit of Christ ,
so that with full heart and voice
we may give glory to God.

May God,
who is the source of hope,
fill us with joy and peace,
so that through the power of the Holy Spirit
we may have unending hope.
May the God of peace be with all of us. †

DH/BASED ON ROMANS 15: 5-6, 13, 33

THAT WE MAY WALK WITH GOD

*W*e pray that God will pour out upon us
the many gifts which reflect God's promise.
May God strengthen us within,
and make a home in our hearts,
with justice and compassion at the center of our lives.
Then we will be able to fully understand
the unbelievable love of Christ,
and to know this love which is beyond our
comprehension,
so that we may walk with God. ✝

DH/BASED ON EPHESIANS 3:16-19

MAY GOD'S PEACE KEEP WATCH OVER US

*M*ay the peace of God,
which is beyond our understanding,
keep watch over our hearts and minds
in Jesus Christ.
Finally, my friends,
all of our thoughts should be
centered on all that is true,
all that is worthy of respect,
all that is honest, pure, decent,
virtuous, or deserving of praise.
May we live according to what
we have learned.
Then the peace of God will
be with us. †

DH/BASED ON PHILIPPIANS 4:7-9

THE GOD OF ALL GRACE

May the God of all grace,
who called us to everlasting glory in Christ,
restore, affirm, strengthen
and establish all who know suffering.
Glory to God forever and ever.

Amen. †

DH/BASED ON I PETER 5:10-11

IRISH BLESSING

May the road rise to meet you,
May he wind always be at your back,
May the sun shine warm upon your face,
May the rains fall soft upon your field,
May God hold you in the palm of his hand. †

GOSPEL KINDRED

*G*ospel kindred,
how I love thee;
tongue nor pen can never say
the very feelings of affection
growing stronger,
day by day.

Together we travel
with the Gospel,
and we bow down
to what is true,
and tell the world
that Christ our Savior
is creating things anew. †

SHAKER HYMN

SUFI BLESSING

*M*ay the blessing of God rest upon us.
May God's peace abide in us.
May God's presence illuminate our hearts,
Now and forevermore. †

COMMON PRAYERS

THE SIGN OF THE CROSS

In the name of the Father,
and of the Son,
and of the Holy Spirit. †

THE LORD'S PRAYER (TRADITIONAL)

Our Father, who art in heaven,
hallowed be thy name;
thy kingdom come;
thy will be done on earth as it is in heaven.
Give us this day our daily bread;
and forgive us our trespasses
as we forgive those who trespass against us;
and lead us not into temptation,
but deliver us from evil.
For the kingdom, the power,
and the glory are yours,
now and forever.

Amen. †

THE LORD'S PRAYER (CONTEMPORARY)

*O*ur Father in heaven,
hallowed be your name,
your kingdom come,
your will be done,
on earth as in heaven.
Give us today our daily bread.
Forgive us our sins
as we forgive those who sin against us.
Save us from the time of trial
and deliver us from evil.
For the kingdom, the power,
and the glory are yours,
now and for ever.

Amen. ✝

THE ABBA PRAYER OF JESUS AND THE BODY OF CHRIST

*G*od,
Abba of all creation,
of the heavens and earth,
you are the source of the singing stars,
you are our loving parent.

We name and honor you for who you are -
Our God who is living,
and beyond our understanding.

May your future be our future,
May your promise be our destiny.

May your word be the ultimate
word in all our disputes;
may you reign in our lives today and everyday.

We implore you to keep us safe,
sustain us with all that we may need to live
as you would have us live.

May the compassion and mercy
that we share with others
be the quality of the compassion
we find in you toward us.

Do not allow
the power of pain and suffering to destroy us,
do not test us beyond our own strength.

Keep us far away
from all that is in conflict with you;
all that is evil,
all that would isolate us from the gift of your love.

We await you,
we sing of the coming of your reign,
we dance to the music of your power,
and we share in the glory that comes from you
and surrounds us.
All this is yours.
Always.

Amen. †

DH/INSPIRED FROM THE LORD'S PRAYER

DOXOLOGY

*G*lory be to the Source of all things!
To Jesus the Christ!
To the Great Spirit!
From our beginnings,
to the time beyond our death;
May light and life never end.

Amen. †

DH/INSPIRED FROM THE GLORIA PATRI

THE BEATITUDES

*B*lest are they, the poor in spirit;
theirs is the Kingdom of God.

Blest are they, full of sorrow;
they shall be consoled.

Blest are they, the lowly ones;
they shall inherit the earth.

Blest are they, who hunger and thirst,
they shall have their fill.

Blest are they, who show mercy;
mercy shall be theirs.

Blest are they, the pure of heart;
they shall see God.

Blest are they, who seek peace;
they are the children of God.

Blest are they, who suffer in faith;
the glory of God is theirs.

Blest are you who suffer hate,
all because of me;
Rejoice and be glad,
yours is the kingdom,
shine for all to see!

Rejoice and be glad!
Blessed are you! Holy are you!
Rejoice and be glad!
Yours is the Kingdom of God! †

DH/THE BEATITUDES - MATTHEW 5:3-10

THE JESUS PRAYER

*L*ord Jesus Christ,
Son of the living God,
have mercy on me, a sinner. †

THIS IS AN ANCIENT EASTERN CHRISTIAN CONTEMPLATIVE PRAYER, DEVEL
OPED FROM THE DESERT FATHERS.

THE TRADITIONAL APPROACH TO THIS PRAYER:

1. TO SIT IN PHYSICAL STILLNESS
2. TO CENTER ONESELF MENTALLY
3. BREATHE DEEPLY
4. FOCUSING:

       LORD JESUS CHRIST (BREATHING IN)

       SON OF THE LIVING GOD (BREATHING OUT)

       HAVE MERCY (BREATHING IN)

       ON ME, A SINNER (BREATHING OUT)

THE "O" ANTIPHONS

O Wisdom,
breath of the most high,
filling all creation;
Come show us how to live!

O Sacred Lord of Israel,
who appeared in the burning bush,
and gave the law on Sinai;
Come stretch out your hand to set us free!

O Flower of Jesse's stem,
every eye is held by you;
all powers bow down before you
to your beauty;
Come to our rescue!

O Key of David,
controlling the gates of heaven;
Come break down the walls of death,
we your captives;
Come, lead us into freedom!

O Radiant Dawn,
splendor of eternal light,
and sun of justice;
Come, shine on us in darkness,
and all in the shadow of death! †

O King of all nations,
the only joy of every human heart;
O Keystone of the mighty arch of time,
come to us;
Save the creature you fashioned from the dust!

O Emmanuel!
God with us!
The nations of the earth
cry out in longing:
Come! Set us free,
our Savior God! †

DH

ETERNAL REST

Eternal rest grant to them, O Lord,
and let perpetual light shine upon them.
May they rest in peace.

Amen. †

COME HOLY SPIRIT

*C*ome Holy Spirit,
fill the hearts of your faithful
and enkindle in them the fire of your love.

V. Send forth your Spirit and they shall be created.
R. And you shall renew the face of the earth.

Let us pray.
O God, who by the light of the Holy Spirit,
did instruct the hearts of your faithful,
grant that be that same Holy Spirit,
we may always be truly wise,
and ever rejoice in your consolation.
Through Christ our Lord.

Amen. †

STATIONS OF THE CROSS

*W*e adore you O Christ and we bless you;
because by your holy cross
you have redeemed the world.

      I. Jesus is condemned to death.
      2. Jesus bears his cross.
      3. Jesus falls the first time.
      4. Jesus meets his mother.
      5. Simon of Cyrene helps Jesus carry his cross.
      6. Veronica wipes the face of Jesus.
      7. Jesus calls a second time.
      8. Jesus meets the women of Jerusalem.
      9. Jesus falls a third time.
    10. Jesus is stripped of his garments.
    11. Jesus is nailed to the cross.
    12. Jesus dies on the cross.
    13. Jesus is taken down from the cross.
    14. Jesus is placed in the tomb. †

EASTER PROCLAMATION

*S*ing with all you have,
all heaven and earth!
All music makers, sing!

All creation,
come and gather around our God!
The Christ is risen!
May the trumpets blast,
and the drums drive us forward
to God's saving way!

Shine bright, O earth!
Christ is victorious!
Glory is ours!
Darkness is destroyed!

Sing loudly, O Church of God!
The one who is risen is here with us!
We cannot contain our joy;
singing and dancing God's wonderful song!

Brothers and sisters,
as we sing in the light of God,
let us call out for mercy,
that we may be worthy
to sing the Easter that has been promised to us.

Alleluia! †

DH/INSPIRED FROM THE OPENING VERSES OF THE EASTER EXULTET

PRAYER OF SAINT FRANCIS

*L*ord, make me an instrument of your peace;
where there is hatred, let me sow love;
where there is injury, pardon;
where there is doubt, faith;
where there is despair, hope;
where there is darkness, light;
and where there is sadness, joy.

Grant that I may not so much seek
to be consoled as to console;
to be understood, as to understand,
to be loved as to love;
for it is in giving that we receive,
it is in pardoning that we are pardoned,
and it is in dying that we are born to eternal life. †

PRAYER OF SAINT PATRICK

*C*hrist be with me, Christ before me, Christ behind me,
Christ in me, Christ beneath me, Christ above me,
Christ on my right, Christ on my left,
Christ where I lie,
Christ where I sit,
Christ where I arise,

Christ in the heart of every one who thinks of me,
Christ in the mouth of everyone who speaks of me,
Christ in every eye that sees me,
Christ in every ear that hears me

Salvation is of the Lord,
Salvation is of the Lord,
Salvation is of the Christ,
May your salvation, O Lord, be ever with us. †

PRAYER OF SAINT IGNATIUS

*T*ake O Lord,
and receive all my liberty,
my memory,
my understanding,
and all my will,
all that I have and possess.
You have given all of these to me;
to you I restore them.
All are yours,
dispose of them all according to your will.
Give me your love and your grace;
having but these I am rich enough
and ask for nothing more. †

HOLY SPIRIT PRAYER OF SAINT AUGUSTINE

Breathe in me, O Holy Spirit,
that my thoughts may all be holy;
Act in me, O Holy Spirit,
that my work, too, may be holy;
Draw my heart, O Holy Spirit,
that I love but what is holy.
Strengthen me, O Holy Spirit,
to defend all that is holy;
Guard me, then, O Holy Spirit,
that I always may be holy.

Amen. †

THE SERENITY PRAYER

*G*od,
grant me the serenity
to accept the things I cannot change,
the courage to change the things I can,
and the wisdom to know the difference. ✝

MARIAN PRAYERS

HAIL MARY

*H*ail Mary, full of grace,
the Lord is with you!
Blessed are you among women,
and blessed is the fruit of your womb, Jesus.
Holy Mary, Mother of God,
pray for us sinners,
now and at the hour of our death.

Amen. †

A PRAYER TO MARY

*Y*ou, Mary,
You are close to God.
You are blest and holy.
You are the bearer of the anointed one,
You are the human source of God walking with us.
You are our Mother as well,
and we cry for your prayer and investment in us
when we falter.
Be with us now,
throughout all our days.

Amen. †

DH/INSPIRED AND BASED ON THE HAIL MARY

THE ANGELUS

The angel of the Lord declared unto Mary
and she conceived by the Holy Spirit.

Hail Mary, full of grace,
the Lord is with you.
Blessed are you among women
and blessed is the fruit of your womb, Jesus.
Holy Mary, mother of God,
pray for us sinners now
and at the hour of our death. Amen.

Behold the handmaid of the Lord.
Be it done unto me according to your word.

Hail Mary...
And the word was made flesh
And dwelt among us.

Hail Mary...
Pray for us, O holy mother of God,
That we may be made worthy of the promises of Christ.

Fill our hearts with your grace, O God:
Through the message of an angel
you have revealed to us the incarnation of your Son;
may his passion and cross
bring us all to the glory of his resurrection.
We ask this through Christ, our Lord.

Amen. †

REGINA CAELI (QUEEN OF HEAVEN)

*R*egina caeli, laetare, alleluia.
Quia quem meruisti portare, alleluia.
Resurrexit sicut dixit, alleluia.
Oro pro nobis Deum, alleluia.

Queen of heaven, rejoice, alleluia.
For he whom thou didst bear, alleluia.
He has risen as he said, alleluia.
Pray for us to God, alleluia. †

MEMORARE

*R*emember, most gracious Virgin Mary,
that never was it known
that anyone who fled to your protection,
implored your help,
or sought your intercession was left unaided.
Inspired by this confidence,
I fly unto you,
O Virgin of virgins, my Mother,
To you I come,
before you I stand,
sinful and sorrowful.
O Mother of the Word incarnate,
despise not my petitions,
but in your mercy hear and answer me.

Amen. †

ATTRIBUTED TO ST. BERNARD OF CLAIRVAUX (1090-1153)

THE MYSTERIES OF THE ROSARY

*T*he Joyful Mysteries:

1. The Annunciation (Luke 1:30-33)
2. The Visitation (Luke 1:50-53)
3. The Nativity (Luke 2:10-11)
4. The Presentation (Luke 2:29-32)
5. The Finding of Jesus in the Temple (Luke 2:48-52)

The Sorrowful Mysteries:

1. The Agony in the Garden (Matthew 26: 38-39)
2. The Scourging at the Pillar (John 19:1)
3. The Crowning with Thorns (Mark 15: 16-17)
4. The Carrying of the Cross (John 19: 17)
5. The Crucifixion (John 19:28-30)

The Glorious Mysteries:

1. The Resurrection (Mark 16: 6-8)
2. The Ascension (Acts 1:10-11)
3. The Coming of the Holy Spirit (Acts 2:1-4)
4. The Assumption of Mary (Song of Songs 2:3-6)
5. The Coronation of Mary (Luke 1:51-54) †

ALSO BY DAVID HAAS

FROM GIA PUBLICATIONS-
MUSIC COLLECTIONS AND RECORDINGS:

- We Have Been Told
- To Be Your Bread
- Psalms for the Church Year, Volume One
      with Marty Haugen
- Come and Journey
      Live Concert with Marty Haugen and Michael Joncas
- Light and Peace
- As Water to the Thirsty
- Who Calls You By Name, Volumes One and Two
- Psalms for the Church Year, Volume Three
- Winter Grace
      Music for Christmas and Wintertime with Jeanne Cotter
- Singing Assembly
      Live Concert with Marty Haugen and Michael Joncas
- Creating God
- I Shall See God
- Table Songs
- How Can I Keep from Singing?
      Live Concert with Jeanne Cotter and Marty Haugen
- When Love Is Found
      Musical and Liturgical Resources for Weddings
- Mass for the Life of the World
- No Longer Strangers
- Where the River Flows
- Blest Are They; The Best of David Haas, Volume One
- You Are Mine: The Best of David Haas, Volume Two

ALSO FROM GIA:

- I Will Call God's Name: The Ministry of Cantor
      A Video Workshop with David Haas and Bonnie Faber

FROM ST. ANTHONY MESSENGER PRESS:

- Psalm Prayers
- The Ministry of Sung Prayer
- Christian Initiation: Liturgical, Catechetical,
    and Musical Dimensions
    David Haas and Thomas H. Morris
    a four cassette audiotape set

GIA Publications, Inc.
7404 South Mason Avenue Chicago, Illinois 60638
708-496-3800

St. Anthony Messenger Press
1615 Republic Street, Cincinnati, Ohio 45210
513-241-5615

FOR WORKSHOP AND
CONCERT BOOKING INFORMATION:

The Emmaus Center for Music, Prayer, and Ministry
2048 Juliet Avenue
St. Paul, Minnesota 55105

ABOUT THE AUTHOR

*D*avid Haas lives in St. Paul, Minnesota, where he is the Director of The Emmaus Center for Music, Prayer and Ministry, a resource network and center for ministry formation. Well known as one of the prominent composers of liturgical music in North America, he has published over 20 collections of music for worship. He has traveled throughout the United States, Canada, Europe, Australia and Israel as a speaker, workshop/retreat leader and concert performer. In 1991, David was nominated for a Grammy Award for the recording of I Shall See God (GIA). He was one of the consultants for the contemporary hymnal, Gather (GIA), and is also the author of Psalm Prayers (St. Anthony Messenger Press).